Clueless in Alaska—Know More!

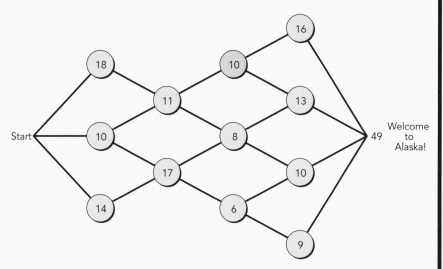

18 — 11 — 10 — 16
10 — 8 — 13
Start — 10 — 17 — 49 Welcome to Alaska!
14 — 6 — 9

The 49th State

Alaska became the 49th state on January 3, 1959. **Can you find your way to Alaska through this maze?** The correct path adds up to 49.

ℱact: "Alaska" is the only state name that can be typed using just one row of letters on a standard computer keyboard.

BLEAT OF STENCONT

Mt. McKinley was called "Denali" by Native Alaskans. It means "the high one." Many Alaskans use the name today.

What's the BIG Deal?

Glad you asked! For starters, Alaska is the biggest state in the USA. Texas comes in a distant second. In fact, if you cut Alaska in half, Texas becomes the third largest state. And that's just the beginning.

Mountains

Alaska is home to Mt. McKinley. At 20,320 feet, it's the tallest mountain in North America. Of the 20 highest mountains in the USA, 17 are in Alaska.

Glaciers

With all those big, snowy mountains, it's no wonder Alaska has about 100,000 glaciers. The Bering Glacier complex is twice the size of Rhode Island. Alaska has more than a quarter of Earth's mountain glacier ice.

Animals

The largest member of the deer family is the moose. The largest moose in the world are in—you guessed it!—Alaska.

The largest group of bald eagles in the world gathers just north of Haines, Alaska, every fall. Over 3,000 eagles come to feast on late-running salmon.

Antlers are biggest when moose are 6–12 years old, and can measure 6 feet from tip to tip.

Fact: Alaska has 47,300 miles of coastline. That's more than all the Lower 48 states put together.

Fact: Alaska has more earthquakes than all the other states combined.

Speaking of salmon, would it surprise you that the largest Pacific king salmon on record was caught in Alaska? Probably not. It weighed 126 pounds. (How much do *you* weigh?)

Another salmon-eater is the coastal brown bear (same species as the grizzly bear). Their protein-rich diet helps these bears grow up to 1,500 pounds, making them the largest omnivorous (meat- and vegetation-eating) land mammal in the world. That is, if you don't count polar bears, because they live on polar ice and not land. Alaska has polar bears, too.

Vegetables

If you're going to have a giant salmon steak or mooseburger, you'll probably want some giant vegetables to go along with it. You'll find them in Alaska. The long summer days (almost 20 hours of sunlight) and mild climate of the Matanuska Valley produce magnificent produce. The prize-winning green cabbage at the 2000 Alaska State Fair weighed—get this—105.6 pounds! The world-record red cabbage, carrot, kale, kohlrabi, beet, broccoli, and Swiss chard were all grown in Alaska.

Nearly 20 hours of sunlight in the summer help vegetables such as cabbage grow to giant sizes.

The Biggest Deal of All

In spite of its grand size, Alaska came with a teeny-tiny price tag. In 1867, Secretary of State William H. Seward convinced Congress to purchase Alaska from Russia for $7.2 million. That's a lot of money, but at a measly two cents an acre, that's got to be the biggest deal of all!

Go the Distance

Alaska has about as many miles of roads as what other state?

Cross off every letter that appears three times in the grid below. Write the remaining letters to answer the question on the line below.

L	V	Y	W	E	A	U
P	C	R	A	L	C	M
O	W	U	L	P	Y	W
N	Y	P	C	T	U	A

_____

Joke: There are more caribou in Alaska than there are people. What is the #1 statewide use of caribou hide?

To hold caribou together.

Alaska has more bald eagles than all the other states combined.

Popular Opinion

Many people thought it was silly to purchase Alaska from Russia. They called it an "ice box," and thought there was nothing there. William H. Seward disagreed. He urged Congress to buy Alaska. **Hold this page in front of a mirror to read what some people called the purchase of Alaska.**

SEWARD'S FOLLY

Coastal grizzly bears that eat a lot of fish grow larger than inland grizzlies that eat mainly vegetation.

ALASKA'S FLAG

The Boy

John Ben "Benny" Benson was born in 1913 in Chignik, a tiny village on one of the Aleutian islands. His mother was Aleut-Russian. His father was a Swedish fisherman. Benny's mother died when he was three, and Benny was sent to live at the Jesse Lee Mission Home, first in Unalaska, then in Seward.

The Challenge

In 1927, the Alaska Department of the American Legion held a flag design contest for students in grades 7–12. Benny drew several designs, but being a seventh-grader, he didn't think he could win.

The Contest

One hundred forty-two designs made it to Juneau for the final contest. Judges chose a simple, but symbolic design: eight gold stars on a field of blue. Seven stars made the constellation Ursa Major, or the Great Bear, also called the Big Dipper. The eighth star was Polaris, the North Star. The message with the flag read:

The blue field is for the Alaska sky and the forget-me-not, an Alaskan flower. The North Star is for the future state of Alaska, the most northerly in the union. The Dipper is for the Great Bear—symbolizing strenth.

Thirteen-year-old Benny Benson created that flag. He worried his entry would be disqualified because he misspelled "strength," but the judges overlooked his mistake.

The Prize

Benny received a gold watch with his design engraved on the back. The Alaska Legislature gave Benny $1,000 so that he could deliver his flag to President Coolidge, but a date could not be arranged. Benny used the money to pay for his education in diesel mechanics instead.

State Symbols

Crack the codes to identify these Alaska state symbols.

Begin at the dot, and read every second letter (puzzles with a 2) or every third letter (puzzles with a 3), clockwise. Write the answer next to the appropriate state symbol. All the letters in the codes are used.

(1)

(2)

(3)

(4)

(5)

(6)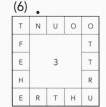

(1) Flower:

(2) Tree:

(3) Bird:

(4) Fish:

(5) Sport:

(6) Motto:

Tufted puffins spend most of
their lives on the open sea.
They visit land only to breed.

Glaciers

Glaciers form when more snow falls than melts. On some mountains in Alaska, the snow never melts, not even in the summer. Year after year, snow piles up. It gets heavy, smooshing the snow on the bottom into ice. Some mountains are covered with giant fields of ice. Eventually, the ice creeps downhill, pulled by gravity.

Hold the page at eye level to read another name for glaciers.

A chunk of ice breaks off Northwestern glacier with a thunderous crack.

Fact: Glaciers cover about 29,000 square miles of Alaska. That's an area almost as big as South Carolina.

Fact: Alaska's 100,000 or so glaciers contain about three quarters of the state's fresh water. The more than 3,000 rivers and 3 million lakes are just one quarter of Alaska's fresh water.

Switcheroo

What animals spend their entire lives on glaciers? **To find out, follow the directions below carefully—*very* carefully!**

1. Write **GLACIERS** in the space provided.

2. Switch the sixth and seventh letters.

3. Switch the second and third consonants.

4. Change the first vowel to **M**.

5. Change the first letter to **O**.

6. Switch the first two vowels.

7. Change the fourth letter to **W**.

8. Switch the third and seventh letters.

Off the Edge

Glaciers begin with snow in the mountains and sometimes end with huge chunks of ice breaking free. **What is it called when chunks of ice break off the end of a glacier?**

Write the answers to each of the clues on the spaces, one letter per space. All the answers rhyme with **snow**. Read down the boxed letters to answer the question above.

As ice fields grow, gravity pulls glaciers downhill. As they creep downhill, they crack, opening crevasses that can be 100 feet deep.

	Clue
☐ ___ ___ ___	Black bird, smaller than a raven.
☐ ___ ___	Woolly mammoths roamed Alaska long _____.
☐ ___ ___	Arctic vegetation is short; it grows _____ to the ground.
P h o t o	What Grandma might make you watch after her trip to Alaska.
I D A H O	State between Washington and Montana.
N O	What your parents will probably say if you ask for a pet moose.
☐ ___ ___ ___	What cabbages do during the long Alaska summer days.

Fact: Icebergs form when chunks of ice break off a glacier into the sea. Up to 80 percent of an iceberg is hidden underwater. What you see really is "just the tip of the iceberg."

Horns & Antlers

Ever seen a moose horn? Bet you haven't. *They don't exist!* (Yeah, that was a trick question.)

Moose, caribou, and all other members of the deer family have antlers. Musk oxen, Dall sheep, and mountain goats have horns.

What's the difference?

Antlers, which are made of bone, usually branch. Only males grow them, and they fall off every winter. New ones grow in the spring. While antlers are growing, they are covered in a soft skin called "velvet." The velvet dries and falls off in the fall. So when you see a moose with antlers as wide as your dad is tall, remember that they grew in less than a year!

Horns are made of keratin. Our fingernails are made of keratin, too. Horns don't branch, both males and females have them (though females' are smaller), and they never fall off. The same set of horns grows bigger each year.

Similarities

Males use their horns or antlers during mating season to attract females and drive off other males. Sometimes just having a big "rack" scares off smaller males. At other times, males fight to see who's bigger and stronger. Moose and caribou lock antlers and push. Sheep and musk oxen charge and bash their horns together. These animals rarely die after a fight. The smaller one usually runs away.

What's the point?

Females prefer strong, healthy males so their young will be strong and healthy, too.

One exception (There's always one.)

Female caribou grow antlers. They are the only female deer to do so.

The "velvet" that covers growing antlers has blood vessels that will dry up as the skin is shed.

Musk ox horns can be 4 inches thick at the base. Along with a 3-inch-thick skull, the horns protect the bull's brain when it crashes heads with another bull.

Joke: Why is it hard to talk to a ram?

He keeps butting in.

JigDraw Puzzle

Copy the red lines of each puzzle piece into the correct square in the grid to make a picture. Correct squares are where the letter and number below each piece meet on the grid. We've done the first one to get you started. **What is this a picture of, and does it have horns or antlers?**

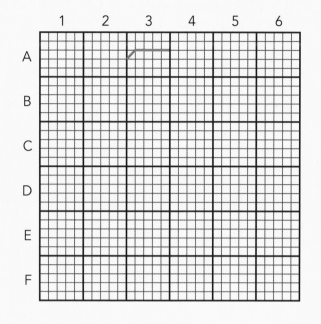

Bull moose lock antlers and "wrestle," unlike sheep, which charge and crash horns.

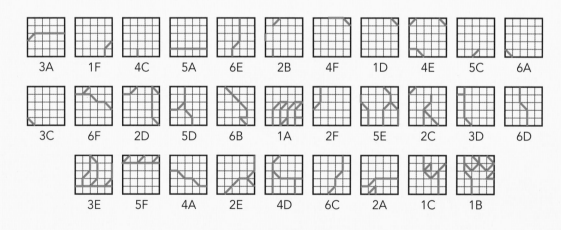

3A	1F	4C	5A	6E	2B	4F	1D	4E	5C	6A
3C	6F	2D	5D	6B	1A	2F	5E	2C	3D	6D
3E	5F	4A	2E	4D	6C	2A	1C	1B		

This Dall sheep's horn is cracked. Horns don't fall off and regrow, so it will remain cracked for the rest of the sheep's life.

Joke: How do you get down off a moose?

You don't. You get down off a duck.

Rivers & Lakes

The Matanuska River is a glacial river, beginning at the Matanuska glacier. Most glacial rivers appear muddy and gray because of the silt they carry. Silt is finely ground rock "flour" that the glacier has scraped out of the mountains.

Top 10 Rivers in Alaska

The Yukon River is the longest of Alaska's more than 3,000 rivers, and the third longest in the USA. The next nine Alaskan rivers in length are listed in the chart below. **Using the clues below, put them in order, 1–9, with 1 being the longest and 9 being the shortest. Write the number for each river on the space provided.**

Innoko	Porcupine	Noatak
_____	_____	_____
Birch Creek	Koyukuk	Kobuk
_____	_____	_____
Kuskokwim	Tanana	Colville
_____	_____	_____

Clues

1. The numbers in the center column add up to 7, and the numbers in the center row add up to 19.

2. Rivers numbered 2, 3, and 8 all start with the same letter.

3. The sum of the numbers in the top row equals the sum of the numbers in the bottom row.

4. River #1 has 9 letters in its name, and river #6 has 1 letter less than river #3.

5. The Noatak River is not as long as the Innoko River.

Sockeye salmon gather in streams and lakes to spawn (lay their eggs).

Almost Anagrams

Alaska has more than 3 million lakes that are at least 20 acres in size. The largest natural freshwater lake is 1,150 square miles—that's bigger than the state of Rhode Island. **What is this giant lake?**

Words in column A have a match in column B. B words have the same letters as the A words, minus 1. For instance, "THIS" would be a match for "SHIRT." It has the same letters, minus 1. The extra letter is "R."

Draw a line connecting matching words, and write the extra letters on the spaces. Read down the extra letters to learn the name of Alaska's largest natural freshwater lake.

	A	B
___	TABLE	BEAST
___	GIANTS	MAP
___	BASKET	NEWT
___	STABLE	LATER
___	GRAIN	SCOUT
___	PALM	STING
___	TWINE	BEAT
___	PARADE	TEST
___	CUSTOM	BLAST
___	ANTLER	RANG
___	TASTE	DRAPE

𝓕act: With 365,000 miles of waterway, Alaska has more river miles than road miles. People travel the rivers by boat in the summer and on snow machine or dogsled in the winter.

Earthquakes & Volcanoes

Alaska is like a jigsaw puzzle made up of pieces of Earth's crust locked together. But some pieces don't fit and are being *forced* together. One giant puzzle piece, the North American tectonic plate, overlaps the Pacific tectonic plate along the southern coast from the Aleutian Islands through southeast Alaska. The results of these pieces smashing together are mountain ranges rising, volcanoes erupting, and earthquakes shaking.

Ready, Set, Blow!

Of all the volcanoes in the world that might erupt, 10% are in Alaska **How many possibly active volcanoes does Alaska have?**

To find out, complete the maze below by adding or subtracting 3 to each number. You can move up, down, left, right, or diagonally. For instance, if you started on 4 (you don't), your next move would be to either 7 (4 + 3) or 1 (4 – 3). Note that you can't go from 6 to 21 or 30 to 21.

		Start						Stop			
10	7	3	8	12	15	18	21	19	24	41	45
13	4	6—21	24	27	30	33	30—21	38	48		
16	9	13	16	18	16	13	27	32	35	24	51
12	7	10	19	22	21	30	9	6	23	20	27
19	15	20	23	24	28	33	42	45	3	18	30
22	25	12	27	25	22	36	15	6	15	53	33
18	9	39	20	24	30	39	9	12	33	50	36
6	21	36	28	25	21	42	33	36	30	47	39
24	9	33	19	18	30	33	45	39	33	42	43
27	30	12	15	22	27	36	39	48	45	46	47

In Pieces

Match the pieces below to the same shapes at the bottom. **Copy the letters into the correct spaces to spell out an earth-shattering fact.**

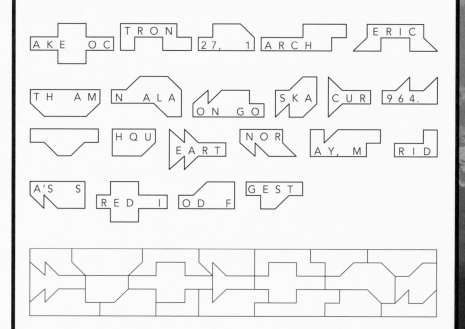

Fact: The greatest volcanic eruption on Earth in the 20th century happened in Alaska. In 1912, Novarupta spewed ash and rocks for 60 hours. Houses 100 miles away collapsed under more than a foot of ash.

The Word on Birds

Millions and millions of birds flock to Alaska in the spring to feast on insects, seeds, berries, fish, and aquatic plants. Alaska's wild lands are perfect for breeding, nesting, and raising young birds.

- Arctic terns log up to 24,000 miles a year. They migrate from Antarctica to the Arctic in spring, then back to Antarctica in the fall.

- Most loons cannot take off from land. Their legs are set far back on their bodies, making them great swimmers, but lousy walkers.

- Snowy owls nest on the ground, and defend their nests from people, wolves, and foxes. They are such good protectors that geese and ducks choose to nest near them.

- After swimming, cormorants spread their wings to dry in the wind and sun. Other sea birds don't have to. Some cormorant feathers are designed for deep diving and don't shed water.

- Puffins sometimes eat so much that they can't get airborne from the water. They're better swimmers than flyers anyway.

Joke: Why do ptarmigan lay their eggs on the ground?

If they dropped them, they would break.

Fact: Of the more than 450 species of birds in Alaska, fewer than a third stay for the winter.

Morse Code

The scientific name for ptarmigan is *Lagopus*. It's a fitting name. Find out what it means by deciphering the Morse code below. Letters are separated by slashes.

Look at the ptarmigan picture above. Can you see why it's a fitting name?

•_ A	_••• B	_•_• C	_•• D	• E	••_• F
__• G	•••• H	•• I	•___ J	_•_ K	•_•• L
___ M	_• N	___ O	•__• P	__•_ Q	•_• R
••• S	_ T	••_ U	•••_ V	•__ W	_••_ X
_•__ Y	__•• Z				

Answer:

•_•/•_/_•••/_•••/••/_

••_•/___/___/_

Bird Search

Circle the 26 Alaska birds in the letters below. They can be forward, backward, up, down, or diagonal. Write the unused letters on the spaces in order from left to right, beginning at the top. Your answer will be a tongue-twister. **Read the saying five times,** *fast!*

Loons are excellent swimmers and can dive to 600 feet when searching for food.

```
          N I L R E M
        W S E M N O O L
          A V E T E R N L N S
      S P R U C E G R O U S E K G
    L I B Y E S O O G G C K S I R
  W A L N B A L D E A G L E S N E S
  N E V A R S J L I N P S L A G A S
  R       W W Y I Z F T G L F T G
          R A A E Y I A K I H E S
          E L N R M T E E S O L A
          V H W R G S N I H R W N
          O D A O T R E P E N O D
          L T U R Y K D G R E L P
          O P U E C G W L A H D L I
          T H L E S K A O M L O E P
          O R E I R R A H G N U W Y E
          C H I C K A D E E G S L H R
```

BALD EAGLE	MAGPIE
CHICKADEE	MERGANZER
DUCK	MERLIN
GOLDEN EAGLE	PLOVER
GOOSE	PTARMIGAN
GRAY JAY	RAVEN
GREAT HORNED OWL	SANDPIPER
GULL	SNOWY OWL
HARRIER	SPRUCE GROUSE
HAWK	SWAN
KESTREL	TERN
KINGFISHER	WARBLER
LOON	YELLOW LEGS

At about 19 inches high, the great gray owl is the tallest owl in Alaska.

Unused letters:

_ _ _ _ _ _ _ _ _ _ _ _ _ _ _ _ _ _ _ _ _ _ _ _

_ _ _ _ _ _ _ _ _ _ _ _ _ _ _ _

Young bald eagles aren't black and white, they are mottled brown. It takes 4–5 years for eagles to mature and develop the black-and-white feathers.

Boreal owls are 8–9 inches tall and weigh just 4–7 ounces.

The Rush is On!

Eureka! Gold was first discovered in Alaska on the Kenai Peninsula in 1848. Until the early 1900s, gold strikes in Juneau, Nome, Fairbanks, and other places lured fortune hunters from all over the country. When one person found gold, others rushed to the area hoping to find more. That's why they were called **gold rushes** and **stampedes**. Towns with stores and hotels sprang up, but were abandoned when the rush was over and folks moved on to other strikes.

Gold can still be panned from some of Alaska's rivers. Dirt and rocks are washed in the water, allowing the heavier gold to settle on the bottom of the pan.

Fact: The largest gold nugget found in Alaska weighed 24½ pounds. It was discovered in 1998 in the Ruby District in northern Alaska.

Crack the Safe

Slippery Sal stole your gold! **Crack this safe to recover your fortune.**

All 16 buttons on this combination lock are pressed once, in a particular order. The final button is marked with an **F**. All others tell you where to move next. For instance, **1D** means you press the button one space down next. **1L** is one space left, **1R** is one right, and **1U** is one up. **What is the first button you must press?**

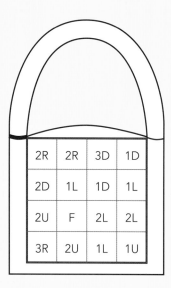

2R	2R	3D	1D
2D	1L	1D	1L
2U	F	2L	2L
3R	2U	1L	1U

To allow year-round mining, a camp and mill were built in 1937 at Independence Mine. Today, the mine is a state historical park.

Your Weight in Gold

Each miner below found a nugget weighing 1, 2, 3, 4, 5, 6, or 7 pounds. No two miners found a nugget the same weight. The number in each circle is the total weight of all the nuggets found by miners whose sections meet at that circle. For instance, the nuggets found by Joe Nome and Klondike Kate add up to 13 pounds. (That's a good place to start, by the way.)

What did each miner's nugget weigh?

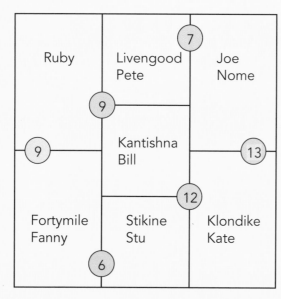

Joke: How do you make gold soup?

Boil 24 karats.

Secret Map

Your partner has struck it rich and needs your help at the claim. He's sent you this map, which is designed to confuse claim jumpers, should it be lost or stolen. You must obey the signs. If an arrow points in one direction, you must continue in that direction until you come to another sign. If there are two arrows in one box, you may choose to go in either direction. If an arrow leads to a dead end, go back and try again. **Can you figure out where your partner is waiting for you—Juneau, Sunrise, Sitka, Nome, Kantishna, or Chisana?**

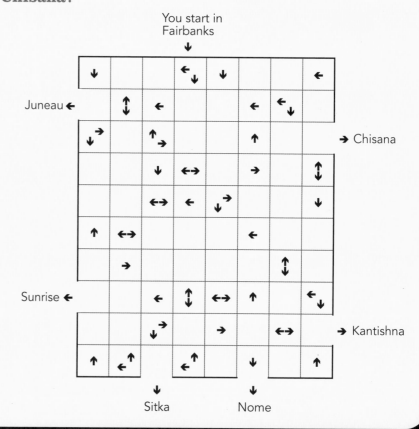

Sea Life

A Steller sea lion bull, cows, and pups warm themselves on a rock.

What's in a Name?

One of Alaska's whales isn't really a whale at all. It's a super-sized dolphin.

Color the triangles—and only the triangles—to see which one it is.

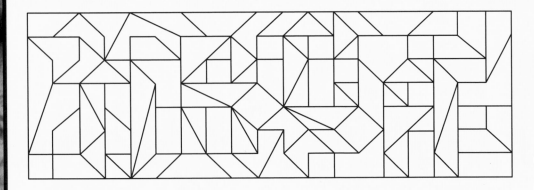

Fact: Sea otters don't have blubber to keep warm. They have super-thick fur. Sea otter fur is what brought Russians to Alaska in the 1800s.

"Kodiak," a sea otter, was rescued after the *Exxon Valdez* oil spill in Alaska. Today he is a favorite at the Oregon Coast Aquarium.

Joke: Why do dolphins swim in salt water?

Because pepper makes them sneeze.

16

Crisscross the Sea

Part 1: Place the 18 sea creatures below into the grid so that they crisscross, as in a crossword. Each word is used once.

4 LETTERS
GULL
ORCA
SEAL

5 LETTERS
MURRE
OTTER
WHALE

6 LETTERS
BELUGA
PUFFIN
WALRUS

7 LETTERS
DOLPHIN
HALIBUT
SEA LION

8 LETTERS
HUMPBACK
KING CRAB
PORPOISE

9 LETTERS
CORMORANT
POLAR BEAR
RAZOR CLAM

Part 2: Write the letters in the numbered boxes on the spaces with the same numbers to read a fascinating fact about Alaska's coastal residents.

‾2‾ ‾14‾ ‾7‾ ‾8‾   ‾5‾ ‾8‾ ‾16‾ ‾1‾ ‾3‾ ‾7‾ ‾4‾ ‾5‾

‾9‾ ‾8‾ ‾5‾ ‾11‾   ‾3‾ ‾9‾   ‾16‾ ‾10‾ ‾16‾ ‾5‾ ‾12‾ ‾16‾

‾11‾ ‾15‾ ‾16‾ ‾9‾   ‾3‾ ‾9‾   ‾16‾ ‾10‾ ‾10‾

‾11‾ ‾15‾ ‾8‾   ‾7‾ ‾8‾ ‾5‾ ‾11‾   ‾14‾ ‾6‾

‾11‾ ‾15‾ ‾8‾   ‾9‾ ‾14‾ ‾7‾ ‾11‾ ‾15‾ ‾8‾ ‾7‾ ‾9‾

‾15‾ ‾8‾ ‾2‾ ‾3‾ ‾5‾ ‾13‾ ‾15‾ ‾8‾ ‾7‾ ‾8‾

Orcas can be identified by their tall dorsal (top) fins. Males' fins are straight and may be as tall as a grown man. Females' fins are shorter and slightly curved.

Joke: What did the king crab yell when he got tangled in seaweed?

Kelp! Kelp!

Dog Sledding

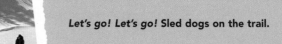

Medicine Run

In 1925 mushers relayed medicine to Nome to save people from a fast-spreading disease. **What was the disease?**

Crack the code to find out. Write a letter on each space that continues the alphabet sequence. It's as easy as A-B-C!

```
F    M    E              B    O    F
G    N    F              C    P    G
H    O    G              D    Q    H

___  ___  ___       ___  ___       ___

E              U    I              B
F              V    J              C
G              W    K              D
```

𝓕𝓪𝓬𝓽: The Iditarod Trail Sled Dog Race is said to be 1,049 miles long. The second half of the number was made up because Alaska is the 49th state. The trail is closer to 1,100 miles.

𝓙𝓸𝓴𝓮: What has a heavy coat in the winter and pants in the summer?

A sled dog.

Mush!

You're going to run the Iditarod. (Not with your sneakers, silly—with dogs!) To a lead dog, "gee" means "turn right" and "haw" means "turn left." **As you race from Anchorage to Nome, follow the directions where the path forks.** If you end up in Nome, you just might have what it takes to be a lead dog!

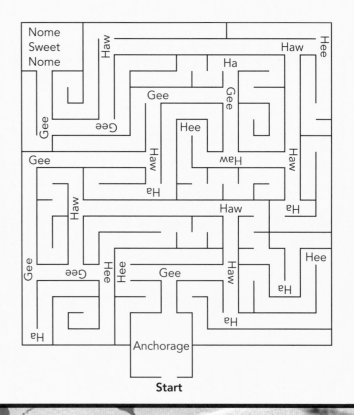

Aurora Borealis (Northern Lights)

Northern lights are streaks of light that swirl, wave, or just sway in the dark northern sky. They are usually green, but can be pink, purple, blue, or red. They are best viewed in the fall and spring.

What causes Northern Lights?

Gases in the sun sometimes explode. A giant explosion can send solar particles out into space. Some of these flow toward the earth, exciting particles in our atmosphere. These excited particles "crash" into gases and give off energy that we see as light.

Why are the lights only in the north?

They're not. They're around the south pole, too, where they're called Southern Lights or Aurora Australis. The earth's magnetic field pulls the solar particles to the poles, the same way it pulls your compass arrow to the pole.

The all-red aurora is a rare treat.

Simon Says

Do what Simon says (and only what Simon says) to discover a fascinating fact about the aurora.

	A	B	C	D	E	F
1	South	Northern	of	Alaska	lights	a
2	occur	Mexico	can	on	summer	heights
3	ago	over	nights	energy	instead	too
4	but	it's	the	Canada	sound	not
5	bites	Florida	dark	kites	enough	until
6	allow	to	is	see	color	them

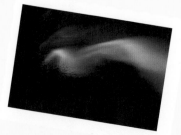

Green is the most common color seen in Northern Lights.

1. Simon says, "Cross off every word in Column F and Row 5 that rhymes with 'lights.'"
2. Simon says, "Cross off every word in Column C with less than four letters."
3. Simon says, "Cross off every word in Row 3 and Column F that starts with a vowel."
4. Cross off every word that contains the letter "T."
5. Simon says, "Cross off every word in Columns B and D that are state or country names."
6. Simon says, "Cross off every word in Rows 1 and 6, and in Column E that have five letters."
7. Simon says, "Read the words that remain in order from left to right, starting at the top."

Plant Life

Tundra

Head north to the arctic and you'll discover land called "tundra." Trees don't grow on the cold and windy tundra. Not much rain or snow falls, and the growing season is short.

It's not easy for plants to grow on the tundra. Ones that do are short and grow close together in "cushions." The temperature in a plant cushion can be 40 degrees warmer than the air one foot above it. Some tundra plants grow "hairs" to hold water and heat. Tundra plants include low shrubs, grasses, moss, flowers, berries, and lichens.

Another place to find tundra is high on mountains, above the treeline. The conditions are different (more rain and not as cold), but the plants are similar.

Fall color on the tundra is on the ground, not in trees.

Boxers

Fit the right boxes into the spaces to complete a fact about Alaska's forests. Black squares are spaces between words, and words wrap from one line to the next.

F		E	S	T	S			V	E			Y		T	O	
N		A		A	S				U	G		N			T	H
R	D		S		T	H	E		T		A	L	A		H	A
S			E		E		F		E			S		B	U		T	H
E		R	C	T	I	C		I	S			L		T	U		R	A

G	I		S	T		O	U		T	■		T	U		O	R		■	D
Y	O		A	L		N	S		N	D		W	A		S	K		■	A

O	R		W	A		A	S
D	R		O	■		O	R

Fact: "Permafrost" is dirt and gravel that is frozen all the time. It's under the thin soil layer in the arctic, and scattered here and there throughout the rest of Alaska.

Coastal forests, full of tall trees, moss, and ferns, get lots of rain.

Lifelines

Fill the boxes with the right letters and names of nine Alaska plants will appear. Boxes that are connected have the same letters. Use logic to guess at others. **Hint:** The plant in the middle is the Alaska state flower.

Fireweed blooms from the bottom of the stalk up. When the top flowers bloom, summer is almost over.

Joke: What did the beaver say to the tree?

Been nice gnawing you.

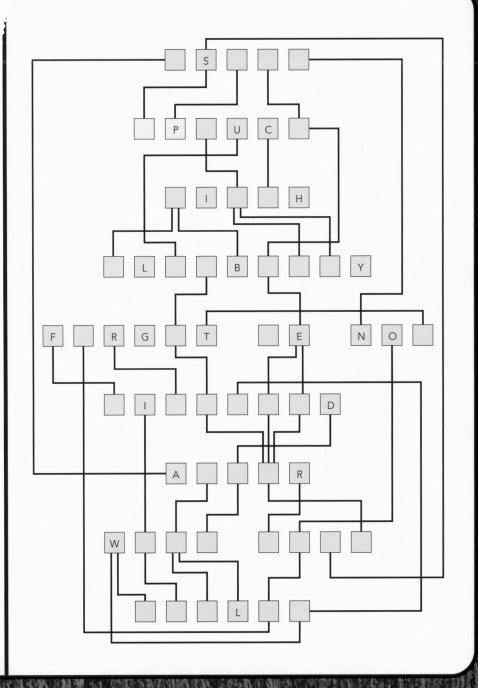

Animals, Animals

Alaska has oodles of animals, but don't expect to bump into a bear behind every bush. The animals are widely spread throughout the state. It takes a lot of tundra to feed a herd of caribou or a grizzly bear. That's because Alaska's plants are not as plentiful or nutritious as some plants elsewhere.

Beaver's Promise

When yesterday was tomorrow, Beaver's father promised, "We'll chew down that big cottonwood the day after tomorrow if it doesn't rain tomorrow and I can patch the lodge roof." It rained the day before yesterday, but has been dry ever since. **Did Beaver and his dad chew down the tree?**

A beaver's incisor teeth never wear out. They keep growing throughout the animal's life.

LQCK TH OQVU

The title above is "CHEW ON THIS" in code. The statement below uses the same code. **Use the letters from the title to begin deciphering the words below. Then use logic and maybe a few guesses to complete the statement.**

KQGO GAGUMG AGLMU VH
——— —————— ————— ——

UBEGYC PCGAU,
—————— —————

VO PGMCU EJ RTY VH
—— ————— —— ——— ——

UBEGYC PVACU.
—————— —————

—Summarized from *The Great Alaska Nature Factbook*, by Susan Ewing

Pikas are members of the rabbit family. They live on rocky slopes high on mountains.

Hidden Animals

Can you find the 24 Alaskan animals in the letters below? They can be forward, backward, up, down, or diagonal. Circle the animals as you find them, then write the unused letters in the spaces to answer this joke:

What Alaskan animal eats with its tail?

```
E X O K S U M L Y N X T
S S H R E W E A S E L H
O C E Y A N R E T T O L
O A L W O D T O O R T H
M R H S O A E M S A S Y
G I I A R L R C Q M H B
N B N K R A V A U N E C
I O S K M E T E I A E O
M U E N I P U C R O P Y
M T A K I E T H R I E O
E M O K B E A V E R N T
L T A O G F W O L F F E
```

Young hares are born with fur and open eyes, unlike rabbits, which are born hairless and blind. Young hares can walk shortly after they're born, and can eat vegetation after two weeks.

BEAR	MOOSE
BEAVER	MUSK OX
BISON	MUSKRAT
CARIBOU	OTTER
COYOTE	PIKA
GOAT	PORCUPINE
HARE	SHEEP
LEMMING	SHREW
LYNX	SQUIRREL
MARMOT	WEASEL
MARTEN	WOLF
MINK	WOLVERINE

Black bears are the smallest of Alaska's bears. They can be black, brown, or cinnamon-colored.

Unused letters: __ __ __ __   __ __ __   __ __.

__ __ __ __   __ __ __ __   __ __ __ __

__ __ __ __   __ __ __!

Marmots live above treeline, digging burrows under rocks on sunny hillsides.

Joke: Where will you find a moose with no legs?

Wherever you left it.

Ptarmigan walk across the snow in search of buds and twigs.

Telltale Tracks

Unscramble the animal names beneath the telltale tracks.

1. FOWL
_____

2. BORUICA
_____

3. RABE
_____

4. GRIMATPAN
_____

5. MAHNU
_____

6. HEAR
_____

7. SOMOE
_____

The front and back feet of bears leave different tracks. The shorter track is from the front paw.

Whodunit?

Ptarmigan's apple pie smelled divine as she set it in the snow to cool on a bright March morning. "Where? . . . What? . . . Who? . . . " she cried, when she returned to fetch her pie. "It's gone!"

Detective Beaver examined the site of the theft. There were four sets of tracks: those of Ptarmigan, Hare, Moose, and Fox. He questioned them all.

"Sure, I saw the pie," said Fox. "And I was sure tempted to have a bite. That snowstorm last night made me miss dinner; I couldn't see a thing and all the voles and hares got away. But I didn't take it. I was hungry for meat, not apples."

"How rude!" exclaimed Moose. "To take someone's pie! But, then, how silly to put a pie out in the snow. It serves Ptarmigan right. Well, it couldn't have been me. I went to Cousin Caribou's last night. It was snowing so hard I spent the night. I came straight home this morning and never saw a pie. I did see Fox tracks. It was probably Fox."

continued on next page

Joke: Why did the goose cross the road?

To get a gander at the other side.

"I . . . I . . . I," stuttered Hare. "I saw Fox tracks, so I got out of there fast. If there was a pie, I didn't see it. I certainly didn't stop to eat it. Gotta run!"

"Oh, dear," said Ptarmigan. "We'd better question Owl. None of these fine animals is a thief."

"I think one of them is," said Detective Beaver after studying the scene of the crime, which is shown on this page.

Who did he suspect and why?

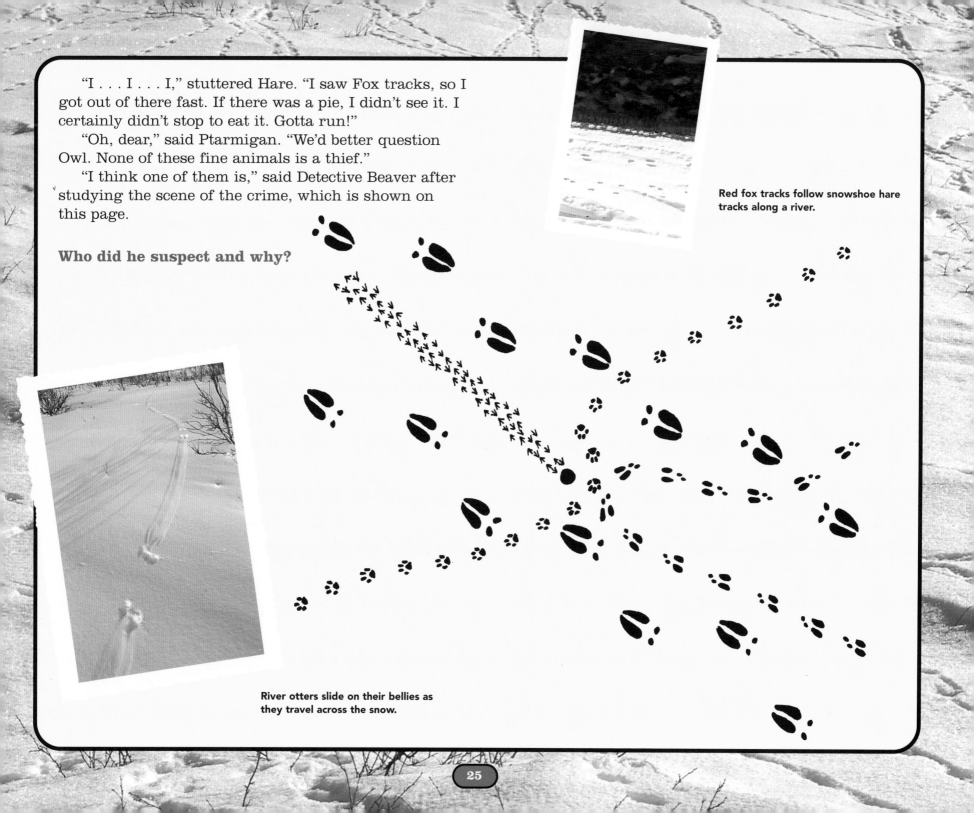

Red fox tracks follow snowshoe hare tracks along a river.

River otters slide on their bellies as they travel across the snow.

25

Fact: With so much land and so few roads it's no wonder Alaska has 6 times as many pilots per capita as the rest of the United States. Alaskans fly a lot.

Fact: There are no roads to Juneau. You can get there by plane or by boat. It's the only state capital you can't drive to.

Hangman

There are six funny Alaska place names hidden in this puzzle. **Try to guess the six place names before you draw a complete hangman on the gallows next to each name.** With every wrong letter guessed, add another body part to your hangman (head, body, two arms, two legs). That gives you six wrong guesses.

1. Choose a letter you think might be in name #1. We've started for you and chosen the letter **A**.
2. Find the symbol on the graph where the chosen letter and puzzle number meet. The symbol for **A** in puzzle 1 is a black circle.
3. If that symbol is in the place name, write the letter above it. **A** *is* in name #1.
4. If the symbol is not in the name, draw the next part of your hangman and write that wrong letter on the space—you don't want to choose it again.
5. Continue guessing letters until you or Hangman wins.

Can you find these places with funny names on a map?

Joke: Why did the king crab cross the road?

To get to the other tide.

	A	B	C	D	E	F	G	H	I	J	K	L	M	N	O	P	Q	R	S	T	U	V	W	X	Y	Z
1	●	□	◆	口	▪	□	✳	✓	#	✚	⋈	~	▯	♥	/	=	⟋	⊥	?	◢	v	ᴔ	☆	ℓ	♣	¢
2	=	#	♣	⟋	ᴔ	/	♥	□	⌘	?	⊥	▪	☆	ℓ	v	~	✚	¢	⋈	✳	◢	口	●	▯	□	
3	☆	¢	✚	~	◢	▯	◆	?	□	∩	=	v	ᴔ	⋈	✳	♥	□	●	ℓ	♣	▪	#	⊥	/	⋈	⟋
4	~	♣	ᴔ	v	✳	●	口	✚	⊥	ℓ	⟋	◢	⋈	☆	▪	□	=	✓	/	⌘	◆	□	▯	∩	#	?
5	◢	/	▪	⋈	¢	□	□	ᴔ	✓	♥	●	#	∩	▯	✚	?	⌘	ℓ	⊥	⟋	♣	=	◆	v	~	✳
6	♥	⟋	ℓ	⊥	▯	#	/	▪	✳	☆	?	◆	□	□	~	●	✓	⋈	v	ᴔ	◢	口	¢	♣	=	✚

Wrong Letters

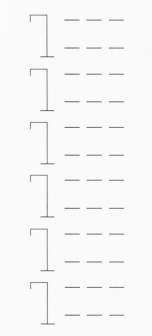

1. __ __ __ __ A __ __ __ __ __
   ⋈ # ♥ ✳ ? ● ~ ▯ / ♥

2. __ __ __ __ __ __ __ __ __
   ⟋ ᴔ = ⟋ □ ℓ ✚ ¢ ᴔ

3. __ __ __ __ __ __ __ __
   ◆ ● ☆ ⋈ v □ 口 ◆

4. __ __ __ __ __ __ __
   ᴔ ✚ ⊥ ᴔ ⟋ ✳ ☆

5. __ __ __ __ __ __
   / ¢ # ♣ □ ◢

6. __ __ __ __ __ __
   ▯ ♥ / ◆ □

Salmon

One Fish/Two Names

There are five species of Pacific salmon found in Alaska: Red, Silver, Pink, King, and Dog. But each of these species has a second name, too. **Use the clues to figure out the second name of each salmon.** Put an X in a box if you can rule it out, and an O in a box that is correct.

	Humpback	Chinook	Chum	Sockeye	Coho
Red					
Silver					
Pink					
King					
Dog					

1. The second name for Chinook (say "shin-OOK"—it rhymes with "book") is not a color.

2. The "man's best friend" salmon has another name that means "friend."

3. Silver salmon are not humpbacks.

4. Sockeyes get their other name because they turn the color of a tomato when they spawn.

Home Sweet Home

Salmon hatch in Alaska's freshwater streams and lakes. Young fish, called "smolts," migrate to the sea. After spending 1–5 years in the ocean, Alaska's salmon return to their home streams to spawn (lay eggs) and die. **How do salmon find their way home?**

To answer that question, look at the letters below. The bottom letters are reflections of the top letters—at least they are *supposed* to be. Circle the letters on the top half that have correct reflections in the bottom half. Read the circled letters to find out how salmon find their way home.

TASMITELGHLT
IＶＳＭＬＩＥＴＧＯＵＴＬ

Dick had a successful day fishing for silver salmon.

Joke: What's the best way to talk with a salmon?

Drop him a line.

27

Native Cultures

Meet Stephanie: Native Dancer

Stephanie (or "Ulaqgak") is an 11-year-old Inupiaq Eskimo. She's been a member of the King Island Dancers and Singers of Anchorage nearly all her life. "I danced when I was 18 months old," she says. Stephanie enjoys performing all over the world. She's danced in Paraguay, Korea, Cincinnati, Seattle, Bethel, Nome, and Fairbanks. "My favorite dance is one my great-grandmother made up." It has no name.

In addition to dancing, Stephanie likes to read. Her favorite school subject is spelling, she likes The Disney Channel, and her favorite foods are walrus and seal—with ketchup. "I only get to eat those when I visit my grandmother in Nome."

Stephanie dances when her father sings.

Fact: What's an orca's favorite game?

Swallow the leader.

Definition Expedition

Find your way to words for these five definitions!

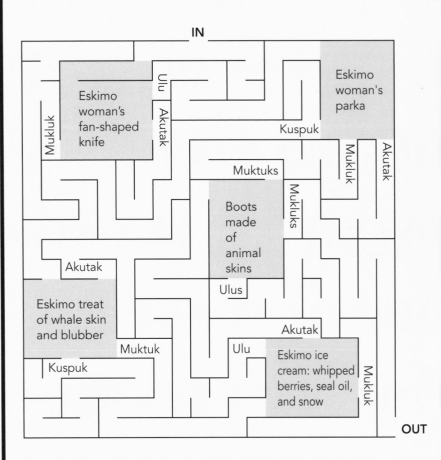

IN

Eskimo woman's fan-shaped knife

Ulu

Akutak

Mukluk

Eskimo woman's parka

Kuspuk

Mukluk

Akutak

Muktuks

Mukluks

Boots made of animal skins

Akutak

Ulus

Eskimo treat of whale skin and blubber

Muktuk

Ulu

Akutak

Kuspuk

Eskimo ice cream: whipped berries, seal oil, and snow

Mukluk

OUT

Joke: Where does a ram get his hair cut?

At a baa-baa shop.

28

Native Peoples

Names of seven Alaska Native groups are listed below. Each name goes into one line in the grid, one letter per box. The given letters are clues to which name goes on which line. There can be empty boxes before and after a name, but not between the letters of a name.

If you place the seven Native groups correctly, the name of an eighth Native group will appear in the outlined column.

Hint: Some names appear to fit on more than one line, but there is only *one* way to fit all of them together.

			S			N	
				I			T
		A	L	E	U	T	
				U		I	
			H			A	
	T						A
		T		I			

ALEUT
ALUTIIQ
ATHABACAN
HAIDA
TLINGIT
TSIMSHIAN
YUPIK

Totem poles, carved by Native Alaskans in southeast Alaska, served many purposes. They represented a family or clan, decorated a house, marked the death of an important person, or symbolized an event.

World Eskimo and Indian Olympics

Every July, Native athletes compete in the World Eskimo and Indian Olympics (WEIO). But you won't see skiing, figure skating, or swimming at these Olympics. The games at the WEIO use skills needed for traditional activities, such as hunting and fishing.

Below are 6 games held at the WEIO. The letters of the games are mixed in with the letters from OLYMPICS. **Cross off the letters that spell OLYMPICS, as in the example, to find the names of the games.**

Example: A R Ø L M Y M P P U I L C S L   ARM PULL

OLSEYALMPHICOPS   [5] __ [8] __   __ __ __

FOOLYURMMAPNICCARSRY   __ [10] __ __ __ __ [6] __   __ __ __ __ __

EAOLRYPUMPLICLS   [3] __ __ __ __ __

DROOLPYTHEMPIBOCMSB   __ __ __ __ [9] __ __ [4] __ __

KNOLEYELMPJUICMPS   __ __ __ __ [2] __ __ __ __

TOOLEYKIMPICCKS   [7] __ __ __   __ __ __ [1]

Write the boxed letters on the spaces with the same numbers to spell the name of a favorite Native event at the Olympics and many other gatherings.

__ __ __ __ __ __ __   __ __ __ __
4   2   8   6   1   3   7   9   10   5   5

Predator & Prey

Camouflage

Four Alaskan animals turn white in the winter. It helps them blend in with the snow, so that predators can't see them.

Vowels from the animals' names have been removed. Can you put them back to reveal all 4 animals?

A A A A A E E E E I I O O O

P T _ R M _ G _ N

_ R C T _ C   F _ X

W _ _ S _ L

S N _ W S H _ _   H _ R _

Joke: What do you call a hare with no hind legs?

Unhoppy.

This fox, hunting a porcupine, better watch out for quills!

Fact: Camouflage helps predators, too. Polar bears sometimes hide their black noses with their paws as they hunt seals.

Martens are the only members of the weasel family to climb trees. They are good hunters, but also eat eggs, berries, and carrion (dead animals).

Connect the Dots!

Ground squirrels are food for just about every predator. Grizzly bears dig giant holes to capture a squirrel in its burrow.

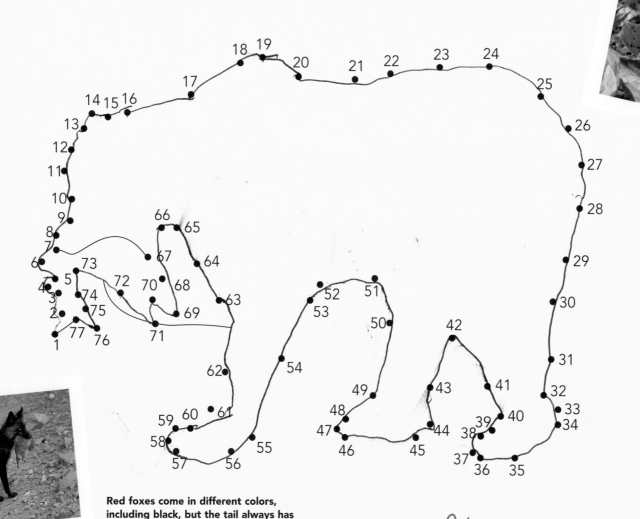

Red foxes come in different colors, including black, but the tail always has a white tip. A vixen (female fox) takes food to the den.

Joke: Why do bears lie on their backs with their feet in the air?

To trip birds.

Animal Babies

Moose twins are not uncommon. Triplets occur on occasion.

Word Windows

Hidden in each group of letters is the name of a baby animal. **Use the windows to reveal the names.** In your mind, place the row of windows on the left over the group of letters on the right. The black squares cover unused letters while the open windows reveal the baby name for that animal.

Young sheep are born in early summer and weigh 5–6 pounds.

Bear	D U **C** K **U** I **B** D	**C U B**
Fox	S K U P E I R T	_____
Swan	C Y A G N W E T	_____
Moose	P C R A M L D F	_____
Wolf	P A C U T O P B	_____
Lynx	K I L T O T E N	_____
Sheep	G L O A M S B Y	_____
Goat	E W E K A B I D	_____
Hare	L E V J E R E T	_____

A young caribou calls for its mother.

Joke: What do moose have that no other Alaskan animals have?

Baby moose.

Young foxes romp near their den.

Twisted Tales

The following stories are missing words. Each space calls for a particular kind of word—a noun, the name of an animal, etc. Without reading the stories first, ask someone (friend, parent, uncle, annoying brother or sister) to give you words to fill in the blanks. **When all the blanks are filled, read the story out loud.**

Noun: person, place, or thing: candy store, bike, chef

Verb: action: jump, wash, knock

Verb, past tense: action that happened before: swam, leaked, flew

Adjective: description: boring, sticky, flat

Exclamation: sound or outcry: Yikes! Egads! Splat!

Plural: more than one: trumpets, flamingoes, shacks

Whoever Gets It, Gets It

A single blueberry remained on the _____ . "It's mine," said _____ .
NOUN   ALASKA ANIMAL #1

"I haven't eaten in _____ ."
PERIOD OF TIME

"Think again,_____ ," said _____ . "I've been watching that
FUNNY NAME   ALASKA ANIMAL #2

_____ berry grow all summer, waiting for it to get_____. It's finally ready, and
ADJECTIVE   ADJECTIVE

I can't wait to _____ it!"
VERB

"Excuse me, _____," said _____, "but you two are
FUNNY NAME, PLURAL   ALASKA ANIMAL #3

_____. _____ shouldn't eat berries. They're bad for your _____ ."
NOUN, PLURAL   SAME NOUN, PLURAL   NOUN

"_____!" said _____.
EXCLAMATION   ALASKA ANIMAL #1

"_____!" said_____.
EXCLAMATION   ALASKA ANIMAL #2

While the three animals argued, _____ _____by and
ALASKA ANIMAL #4   VERB, PAST TENSE

_____ the berry. "_____ ," she said. "Nothing like a _____
VERB, PAST TENSE   EXCLAMATION   ADJECTIVE

blueberry before I_____for the winter."
VERB

Joke: *Sister Smartypants:* What's the capital of Alaska?
Brainy Brother: Juneau.
Sister Smartypants: Of course I know. Do you?

Alaska Extremes

Alaska is a _____ of extremes. Besides being the largest

        NOUN

_____, it also has some of the largest _____ , _____ ,

NOUN   **NOUN, PLURAL**   **ANIMAL, PLURAL**

and _____ . Yet tiny _____ grow on the

      VEGETABLE, PLURAL   **NOUN, PLURAL**

tundra, and itty-bitty _____ live on glaciers. Alaska has

                   ANIMAL, PLURAL

many _____ , but few _____ . In summer it's hard

     NOUN, PLURAL   **NOUN, PLURAL**

to _____ with all the _____ , while in winter it's _____

   VERB   **NOUN**   **ADJECTIVE**

and _____ most of the time. It all adds up to one extremely

    ADJECTIVE

_____ place to live or visit.

  ADJECTIVE

Caribou use their hooves to dig through snow in search of lichens and other winter food.

Joke: How do you catch a unique hare?
How do you catch a tame hare?

"Unique" up on it. / Tame way.

Alaska Rumination

Largest in the nation
Fauna observation
Night illumination
Tourist destination

Highest elevation
Summit aspiration
Snow accumulation
Mountain glaciation

Native corporation
Bush plane aviation
Arctic conservation
Tundra vegetation

Spring and fall migration
Eagle congregation
Fish exaggeration
Goose egg incubation

Oil exploration
Gold anticipation
Mammoth excavation
Cabbage cultivation

Extra large crustacean
Bull moose confrontation
Insect aggravation
Winter hibernation

Alaska Hiking Guide

When hiking in Alaska be prepared. Sturdy _____ will provide good traction and _____ support.
NOUN, PLURAL   BODY PART

Take _____ in case the weather changes. A _____ and _____ will protect
ADJECTIVE NOUN, PLURAL   NOUN   NOUN

you from _____ , and don't forget _____ repellent. There's nothing more annoying
ADJECTIVE NOUN   ALASKA ANIMAL #1

than _____ buzzing and _____ while you're eating _____ .
ALASKA ANIMAL #1, PLURAL   VERB ENDING IN -ING   NOUN

_____ are handy for spotting _____ in the distance, and a good _____
NOUN, PLURAL   ALASKA ANIMAL #2, PLURAL   NOUN

book can help you identify things you see. Make sure you bring lots of _____ to keep you hydrated, and tell
LIQUID

_____ where you're going and when you expect to be back.
SOMEONE YOU KNOW

Be _____ . Be _____ . Have _____ .
ADJECTIVE   ADJECTIVE   NOUN

Because caribou are herd animals, they must keep moving to find food. A herd could strip an area bare if it stayed in one place.

Joke: Why do wolves eat raw meat?

They're lousy cooks.

Alaska Lingo

What's the Meaning of This?

Match the six Alaskan terms below with their meanings. The maze will show you the way.

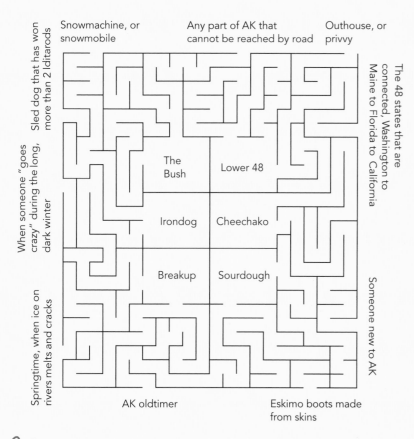

Sled dog that has won more than 2 Iditarods

Snowmachine, or snowmobile

Any part of AK that cannot be reached by road

Outhouse, or privvy

When someone "goes crazy" during the long, dark winter

The 48 states that are connected, Washington to Maine to Florida to California

The Bush

Lower 48

Irondog

Cheechako

Breakup

Sourdough

Springtime, when ice on rivers melts and cracks

Someone new to AK

AK oldtimer

Eskimo boots made from skins

Joke: How do you get a sheep's attention?

Shout, "Hey, Ewe!"

Long Nights/Long Days

In Barrow, Alaska's northernmost town, the sun sets in mid-November and doesn't rise until January. Now that's an Alaska-sized night! In summer, the sun comes up in mid-May, and doesn't set until early August. Other parts of Alaska are not quite so dramatic: Fairbanks gets about 4 hours of daylight in the winter and 22 in the summer. Juneau gets about 6½ hours in the winter and 18½ hours in the summer.

This happens because the earth is tilted on its axis. In winter, the north pole is tilted away from the sun. Even as the earth rotates through days and nights, the pole gets no direct sunlight. In summer, the north pole is tilted toward the sun, giving polar regions 24-hour sunlight.

Alaska has a nickname because of its long summer days. **Hold the page at eye level to read the name below.**

Insects

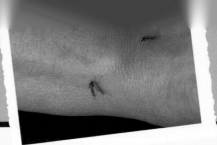

Beetles • Bees • Butterflies • Flies • Midges

Mites • Mosquitoes • Springtails • Wasps

- Only female mosquitoes bite. They need the nutrients in blood to lay eggs.

- Both males and females eat plant nectar.

- Female whitesox (black flies) bite off a chunk of skin and lap up the blood.

- Some Alaska butterflies have a natural "antifreeze" that protects their bodies as they wait out winter in a sort of suspended animation.

- The Alaska state insect is the four-spot skimmer dragonfly.

Funny Buzzzzness

The answer to this joke is "the mosquito." **You figure out the question. Remember, it's a joke!** Follow the instructions and use the letters and numbers in Workbox 1 to fill the empty boxes in Workbox 2.

Workbox 1

0	1	2	3	4	5	6	7	8	9
a	b	c	d	e	f	g	h	i	j

Workbox 2

△	△	⚔	●	■	■	●	⚔	⚔	■	⚔	●	●	■	⚔	●	●	●	●	⚔	●	△	⚔	●	■	⚔	⚔

— — — — — — — — — — — — — — — — — —

1. Subtract the number above g from the number above j, and write the answer in the first, seventh, and twenty-fifth empty boxes from the left in Workbox 2.

2. Divide i by e, and write the answer in the two middle boxes.

3. Add e to f, then divide by three. Write the answer in the tenth and twelfth boxes from the right.

4. Subtract d from h and multiply by b. Write the answer in the eighteenth, twentieth, twenty-first, and twenty-sixth boxes from the left.

5. Subtract c from i and divide by g. Write the answer four times: in the boxes beneath the second triangle and second square from the left, and in the boxes beneath the first square and first circle from the right.

6. Multiply b by c and add a. Write the answer in the third, ninth, and eleventh boxes from the left, and the eighth box from the right.

7. Add g and h, then subtract j. Write the answer in the seventeenth and twenty-third boxes from the right.

8. Subtract one from the above answer and write the new answer in the box left of the middle two boxes.

9. On the spaces below Workbox 2, write the letters where the symbols and numbers intersect in the Answer Key. You will spell out the joke that goes with the answer at the beginning of the puzzle.

10. Check your answer. If you got it right, shout "I did it!" really loud. Then go get a drink and put your feet up—you must be exhausted!

Key

	⚔	●	△	■
1	G	B	H	I
2	A	N	P	K
3	R	S	W	O
4	D	T	E	L

Winter

A fox uses its tail to keep warm during winter.

- **Lowest temperature:** -80°F, Prospect Creek Camp in 1971.
- **Average January temperature in Anchorage:** 15°F.
- **Most snow in a year:** 974.5 inches, Thompson Pass. (That's more than 81 feet!)
- **Most snowfall in 24 hours:** 62 inches, Thompson Pass.

Animal Survival

Winter in Alaska can be windy, cold, and dark. How do the animals stand it?

- Most birds migrate.
- Bears, ground squirrels, and marmots hibernate.
- Moose have long legs to get through deep snow.
- Chickadees roost in groups to keep each other warm.
- Hares grow thick fur on their feet. It helps them hop across the snow. (Think snowshoes!)
- Mice and shrews live in groups under the snow. It's warmer under the snow than above it.

Ptarmigan blend with snow in the winter. They also burrow into it to keep warm.

Tele-Joke

What are the four seasons in Alaska?

The answer to this joke is coded. Each number stands for one of the letters found with it on the telephone. You determine which one. A number may represent a different letter each time it's used. For instance, the code for **high** would be **4444**.

1	ABC 2	DEF 3
GHI 4	JKL 5	MNO 6
PQR 7	STU 8	VWX 9
*	YZ 0	#

5 8 6 3, 5 8 5 0, 2 8 4 8 8 8, 2 6 3   9 4 6 8 3 7

___ ___ ___ ___ ___

Joke: Which side of the musk oxen has the most hair?

The outside.

Alaska A–Z

C How Much You Know!

Each letter of the alphabet is used in one square. **If you put the right letter in the right square, a word relating to Alaska will appear. Cross off the letters as you use them.** We've done one to get you started. Can you do the rest?

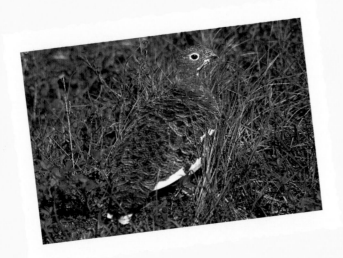

Camouflage helps a ptarmigan hide from predators.

A B C D E F G H I J K L M N O P Q R S T U V W X Y Z

E	A	R	T	H	**Q**	U	A	K	E	R
B	U	R	G	L		A	W	H	A	M
E	S	P	A	R		T	I	C	W	A
H	O	S	A	L		O	N	I	K	E
A	L	B	E	A		E	R	I	C	F
L	E	M	O	O		E	O	E	P	U
M	A	F	I	R		W	E	E	D	X
W	I	G	P	I		U	N	E	A	U
B	A	G	R	I		Z	L	Y	E	S
W	I	S	M	N		M	E	L	F	D
P	R	O	G	L		C	I	E	R	N
C	A	B	B	A		E	L	I	D	M
G	R	M	U	S		O	X	A	L	L
U	Q	U	S	T		N	D	R	A	P
J	A	L	O	O		N	Y	A	R	N
V	B	F	R	C		G	N	E	T	V
F	U	R	A	U		O	R	A	M	S
K	D	A	Y	L		G	H	T	R	J
O	S	L	E	D		O	G	R	U	G
D	R	H	Y	U		I	K	X	N	E
N	O	S	N	O		S	H	O	E	T
V	E	L	V	E		E	R	I	S	G
B	E	N	N	Y		E	N	S	O	N
R	A	L	Y	N		S	M	U	D	G
C	B	E	A	G		E	O	W	E	N
S	M	U	P	U		F	I	N	O	Z

Puzzle Answers

The 49th State

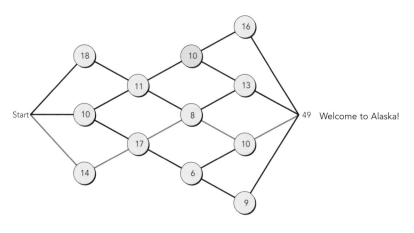

Start · 49 Welcome to Alaska!

Go the Distance
Vermont

Popular Opinion
Seward's Folly

State Symbols
Flower: Forget-me-not
Tree: Sitka spruce
Bird: Willow ptarmigan
Fish: King salmon
Sport: Dog mushing
Motto: North to the Future

Glaciers
Rivers of Ice

Switcheroo
Ice Worms

Off the Edge
Crow, Ago, Low, Video, Idaho, No, Grow:
CALVING

JigDraw Puzzle
This is a mountain goat. It has horns.

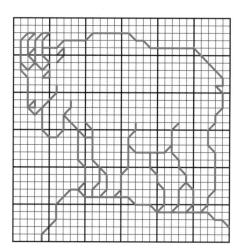

Top 10 Rivers in Alaska

The actual lengths of Alaska's rivers are open to debate. Opinions vary on where rivers begin and end, and how much they meander. According to the *Alaska Almanac*, the 10 longest rivers in Alaska are:

Yukon: 1,400 miles in Alaska, 600 in Canada
Porcupine: 555 miles
Koyukuk: 554 miles
Kuskokwim: 540 miles
Tanana: 531 miles
Innoko: 463 miles
Colville: 428 miles
Noatak: 396 miles
Kobuk: 396 miles
Birch Creek: 314 miles

Innoko	Porcupine	Noatak
5	1	7
Birch Creek	Koyukuk	Kobuk
9	2	8
Kuskokwim	Tanana	Colville
3	4	6

Almost Anagrams

L	TABLE—BEAT
A	GIANTS—STING
K	BASKET—BEAST
E	STABLE—BLAST
I	GRAIN—RANG
L	PALM—MAP
I	TWINE—NEWT
A	PARADE—DRAPE
M	CUSTOM—SCOUT
N	ANTLER—LATER
A	TASTE—TEST

Lake Iliamna (say "ILL-ee-AHM-na")

Ready, Set, Blow!

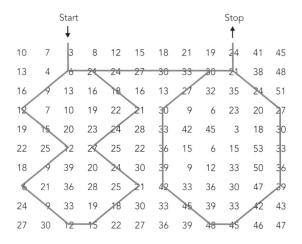

In Pieces

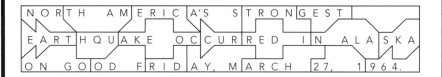

NORTH AMERICA'S STRONGEST EARTHQUAKE OCCURRED IN ALASKA ON GOOD FRIDAY, MARCH 27, 1964.

Morse Code

Lagopus means "rabbit foot."

Puzzle Answers

Bird Search

Seven slick swans slip swiftly through the slough. ("Slough" rhymes with "grew." It is a marshy place.)

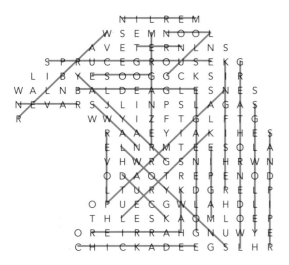

Crack the Safe

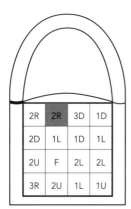

Your Weight in Gold

1—Livengood Pete
2—Stikine Stu
3—Kantishna Bill
4—Fortymile Fanny
5—Ruby
6—Joe Nome
7—Klondike Kate

Secret Map

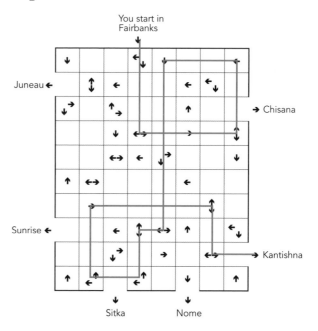

Puzzle Answers

What's in a Name?

An orca is also called a "killer whale." "Whale" is part of its name, though it's not a whale at all. But who's going to argue?!

Crisscross the Sea

Part 1:

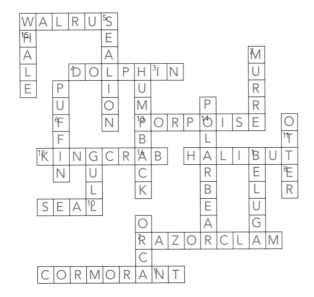

Part 2:

More seabirds nest in Alaska than in all the rest of the northern hemisphere.

Medicine Run

Diphtheria

Mush!

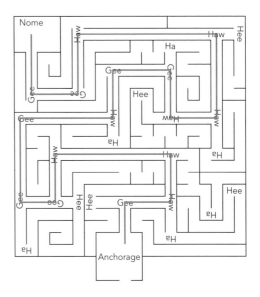

Simon Says

Northern lights occur on summer nights, too, but it's not dark enough to see them.

Boxers

Forests give way to tundra as you go northward. Southeast Alaska has dense forests, but the arctic is all tundra.

Puzzle Answers

Lifelines

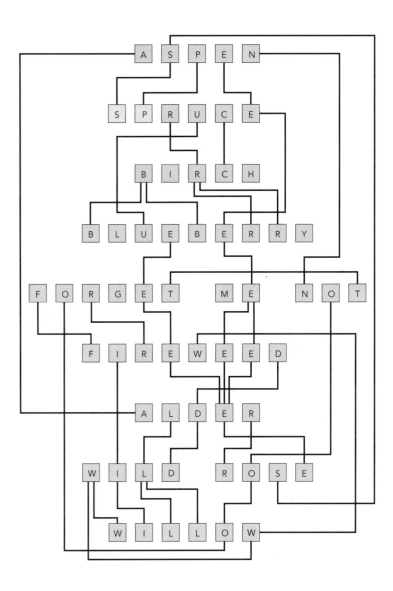

Beaver's Promise

Yes, they chewed it down today.

LQCK TH OQVU

What Alaska lacks in square meals, it makes up for in square miles.

Hidden Animals

They all do. They can't take them off!

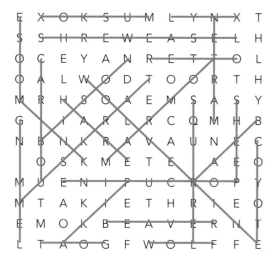

Telltale Tracks

1. Wolf
2. Caribou
3. Bear
4. Ptarmigan
5. Human
6. Hare
7. Moose

Puzzle Answers

Whodunit?

Beaver brought Moose in for further questioning. If she had spent the night at Caribou's and come straight home this morning, she would have left just one set of tracks. Last night's tracks would have been covered with new snow from the storm.

Moose had two sets of tracks past the pie. She was lying.

"Yes! I ate the pie!" Moose confessed.

"You don't know what it's like to eat nothing but dry old branches all winter long."

"Don't I?" asked Detective Beaver.

Hangman

1. King salmon
2. Deadhorse
3. Grayling
4. Chicken
5. Beluga
6. Eagle

One Fish/Two Names

Red—Sockeye
Silver—Coho
Pink—Humpback
King—Chinook
Dog—Chum

Home Sweet Home

Salmon find their way home using their sense of SMELL.

Definition Expedition

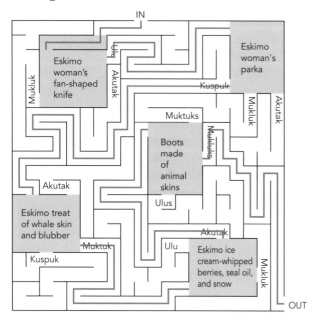

Native Peoples

I N U P I A Q

World Eskimo and Indian Olympics

Seal Hop, Four Man Carry, Ear Pull, Drop the Bomb, Kneel Jump, Toe Kick, Blanket Toss

Camouflage

Ptarmigan
Arctic Fox
Weasel
Snowshoe Hare

Puzzle Answers

Connect the Dots!

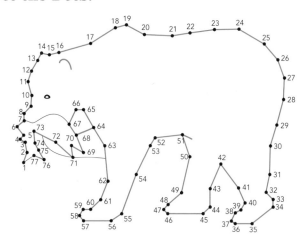

Word Windows

Fox—Kit	Lynx—Kitten
Swan—Cygnet	Sheep—Lamb
Moose—Calf	Goat—Kid
Wolf—Pup	Hare—Leveret

What's the Meaning of This?

Snowmachine, or snowmobile

Any part of AK that cannot be reached by road

Outhouse, or privvy

The 48 states that are connected, Washington to Maine to Florida to California

When someone "goes crazy" during the long, dark winter

Springtime, when ice on rivers melts and cracks

Someone new to AK

AK oldtimer

Eskimo boots made from skins

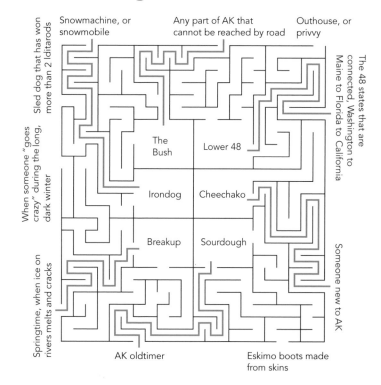

The Bush

Lower 48

Irondog

Cheechako

Breakup

Sourdough

Sled dog that has won more than 2 Iditarods

Long Nights/Long Days
Land of the Midnight Sun

Funny Buzzzzness
What is Alaska's state bird?
The mosquito.

Tele-Joke
June, July, August, and winter.

Alaska A–Z: C How Much You Know!

```
E A R T H Q U A K E R   R
B U R G L H A W H A M
E S P A R C T I C W A
H O S A L M O N I K E
A L B E A V E R I C F
L E M O O S E O E P U
M A F I R E W E E D X
W I G P I J U N E A U
B A G R I Z Z L Y E S
W I S M N O M E L F D
P R O G L A C I E R N
C A B B A G E L I D M
G R M U S K O X A L L
U Q U S T U N D R A P
J A L O O N N Y A R N
V B F R C Y G N E T V
F U R A U R O R A M S
K D A Y L I G H T R J
O S L E D D O G R U G
D R H Y U P I K X N E
N O S N O W S H O E T
V E L V E T E R I S G
B E N N Y B E N S O N
R A L Y N X S M U D G
C B E A G L E O W E N
S M U P U F F I N O Z
```

Thank you, puzzle testers: Zeb, Wayne, Alex, Elliott, Sydonia, Polly, and the fourth-graders from Scottish Corners Elementary School in Dublin, Ohio, especially Miss Dingle's class. Thanks to the Oregon Coast Aquarium for the opportunity to photograph sea otters and puffins. Thanks to Stephanie for dancing. And thank you Dale, Chrissie, Linda C., Mary Beth, and Linda S. for heaps of help and encouragement.

Text and puzzles ©2006 by Jennifer Funk Weber
Photography ©2006 by Mike Weber

Printed in China
Published by Sasquatch Books
Distributed by Publishers Group West
15 14 13 12 11 10 09 08 07 06   6 5 4 3 2 1

Cover and interior design: doublemranch.com

Library of Congress Cataloging-in-Publication Data is available.
ISBN: 1-57061-441-5

Sasquatch Books
119 South Main Street, Suite 400
Seattle, WA 98104
(206) 467-4300
www.sasquatchbooks.com
custserv@sasquatchbooks.com